The Passion Readings for Three Voices

THE
PASSION READINGS
FOR THREE VOICES

JB VERSION

LONDON
DARTON, LONGMAN & TODD

First published in Great Britain in 1972 by
Darton, Longman & Todd Limited
85 Gloucester Road, London SW7 4SU
Reprinted 1972, 1974 and 1977

The Jerusalem Bible © 1966, 1967 and 1968
by Darton, Longman & Todd Ltd and
Doubleday & Company Inc.
Printed in Great Britain by litho
at The Anchor Press Ltd and bound
by Wm Brendon & Son Ltd
both of Tiptree, Essex

ISBN 0 232 51171 3 (cased)
0 232 51172 1 (paper)

Contents

In this book, the Passion narratives of the four Evangelists, Matthew, Mark, Luke and John, are printed in that order. Each one is arranged for reading by three voices, according to the traditional method in the Liturgy. The *Narrator's part* is marked as such: N; *the words of Christ* are marked with ✠; the third reader's part, comprising *the speeches of all other persons*, is marked with **C**. For the convenience of those churches in which any words *spoken by several speakers at once* are read or recited by a choir or the congregation, these are distinguished in this book by the use of brackets round the **C**: [**C**].

It should be noted that the Passion read on the Sunday before Easter in Year 1, begins at Matthew **26**:14 (the verse is marked in the book), and not at the beginning of the Chapter. Similarly, the Passion read on the Sunday before Easter in Year 3, begins at Luke **22**:14, and not at the beginning of the Chapter.

The Short Versions which are permitted in certain circumstances in all three years are noted under the heading of each of the Passions and their first and last verses are marked in the margin.

THE USE OF THIS BOOK IN THE CHURCH OF ENGLAND

The Book of Common Prayer provides for the reading of the Passions as follows:

Palm Sunday	Matthew 27:1–54	(both verses marked in margin)
Monday in Holy Week	Mark 14:1–72	,, ,, ,, ,, ,,
Tuesday in Holy Week	Mark 15:1–39	,, ,, ,, ,, ,,
Wednesday in Holy Week	Luke 22:1–71	,, ,, ,, ,, ,,
Maundy Thursday	Luke 23:1–55	,, ,, ,, ,, ,,
Good Friday	John 19:1–37	,, ,, ,, ,, ,,

The Experimental Lectionary, 1970, provides for the reading of the Passion as follows:

Both Years:	Palm Sunday	Mark 14:1 to 15:39
	Good Friday	John 18:1 to 19:37
Year 1:	Monday in Holy Week	Matthew 26:1–30
	Tuesday in Holy Week	Matthew 26:31–75
	Wednesday in Holy Week	Matthew 27:1–54
Year 2:	Monday in Holy Week	Luke 22:1–38
	Tuesday in Holy Week	Luke 22:39–71
	Wednesday in Holy Week	Luke 23:1–47

In the Revised Lectionary of the Church of the Province of South Africa, the Passion on Palm Sunday is Matthew 26:1 to 27:61.

All the above verses are marked in the margin.

The Passion of Our Lord Jesus Christ According to Matthew

CHAPTER 26, VERSES 1–13*

N   Jesus had now finished all he wanted to say, and he told his disciples,

✠   **It will be Passover, as you know, in two days' time, and the Son of Man will be handed over to be crucified.**

N   Then the chief priests and the elders of the people assembled in the palace of the high priest, whose name was Caiaphas, and made plans to arrest Jesus by some trick and have him put to death. They said, however,

[C]   **It must not be during the festivities; there must be no disturbance among the people.**

N   Jesus was at Bethany in the house of Simon the leper, when a woman came to him with an alabaster jar of the most expensive ointment, and poured it on his head as he was at table. When they saw this, the disciples were indignant, and they said,

[C]   **Why this waste? This could have been sold at a high price and the money given to the poor.**

N   Jesus noticed this and he said to them

✠   **Why are you upsetting the woman? What she has done for me is one of the good works indeed! You have the poor with you always, but you will not always have me. When she poured this ointment on my body, she did it to prepare me for burial. I tell you solemnly, wherever in all the world this Good News is proclaimed, what she has done will be told also, in remembrance of her.**

* Used in the Church of England as Introduction to the Passion.

THE PASSION OF OUR LORD
JESUS CHRIST
ACCORDING TO MATTHEW

[Short version: 27:11—27:54]

N   Then one of the Twelve, the man called Judas **26:**14 Iscariot, went to the chief priests and said

C   **What are you prepared to give me if I hand him over to you?**

N   They paid him thirty silver pieces, and from that moment he looked for an opportunity to betray him.

     Now on the first day of Unleavened Bread the disciples came to Jesus to say,

[C]   **Where do you want us to make the preparations for you to eat the passover?**

N   He replied,

✠   **Go to so-and-so in the city and say to him, 'The Master says: My time is near. It is at your house that I am keeping Passover with my disciples'.**

N   The disciples did what Jesus told them and prepared the Passover.

     When the evening came he was at table with the twelve disciples. And while they were eating he said,

✠   **I tell you solemnly, one of you is about to betray me.**

N   They were greatly distressed and started asking him in turn,

C   **Not I, Lord, surely?**

N He answered,

✠ Someone who has dipped his hand into the 26:23 dish with me, will betray me. The Son of Man is going to his fate, as the scriptures say he will, but alas for that man by whom the Son of Man is betrayed! Better for that man if he had never been born!

N Judas, who was to betray him, asked in his turn,

C Not I, Rabbi, surely?

N Jesus answered,

✠ They are your own words.

N Now as they were eating, Jesus took some bread, and when he had said the blessing he broke it and gave it to the disciples and said,

✠ Take it and eat; this is my body.

N Then he took a cup, and when he had returned thanks he gave it to them saying,

✠ Drink all of you from this, for this is my blood, the blood of the covenant, which is to be poured out for many for the forgiveness of sins. From now on, I tell you, I shall not drink wine until the day I drink the new wine with you in the kingdom of my Father.

N After psalms had been sung they left for the Mount 26:30 of Olives.
　 Then Jesus said to them,　　　　　　　　　　26:31

✠ You will all lose faith in me this night, for the scripture says: I shall strike the shepherd and the sheep of the flock will be scattered. But after my resurrection I shall go before you to Galilee.

12

N   At this, Peter said,

C   **Though all lose faith in you, I will never lose faith.**

N   Jesus answered him,

✠   **I tell you solemnly, this very night, before the cock crows, you will have disowned me three times.**

N   Peter said to him,

C   **Even if I have to die with you, I will never disown you.**

N   And all the disciples said the same.
    Then Jesus came with them to a small estate called Gethsemane; and he said to his disciples,

✠   **Stay here while I go over there to pray.**

N   He took Peter and the two sons of Zebedee with him. And sadness came over him, and great distress. Then he said to them,

✠   **My soul is sorrowful to the point of death. Wait here and keep awake with me.**

N   And going on a little further he fell on his face and prayed,

✠   **My Father, if it is possible let this cup pass me by. Nevertheless, let it be as you, not I, would have it.**

N   He came back to the disciples and found them sleeping, and he said to Peter,

✠   **So you had not the strength to keep awake with me one hour? You should be awake, and praying not to be put to the test. The spirit is willing, but the flesh is weak.**

13

N   Again, a second time, he went away and prayed: **26:42**

✠   **My father, if this cup cannot pass by without my drinking it, your will be done!**

N   And he came again back and found them sleeping, their eyes were so heavy. Leaving them there, he went away again and prayed for the third time, repeating the same words. Then he came back to the disciples and said to them,

✠   **You can sleep on now and take your rest. Now the hour has come when the Son of Man is to be betrayed into the hands of sinners. Get up! Let us go! My betrayer is already close at hand.**

N   He was still speaking when Judas, one of the Twelve, appeared, and with him a large number of men armed with swords and clubs, sent by the chief priests and elders of the people. Now the traitor had arranged a sign with them. He had said,

C   **'The one I kiss, he is the man. Take him in charge.'**

N   So he went straight up to Jesus and said,

C   **Greetings, Rabbi,**

N   and kissed him. Jesus said to him,

✠   **My friend, do what you are here for.**

N   Then they came forward, seized Jesus and took him in charge. At that, one of the followers of Jesus grasped his sword and drew it; he struck out at the high priest's servant, and cut off his ear. Jesus then said,

✠   **Put your sword back, for all who draw the sword will die by the sword. Or do you think**

that I cannot appeal to my Father who would 26:53
promptly send more than twelve legions of
angels to my defence? But then, how would
the scriptures be fulfilled that say this is the
way it must be?

N   It was at this time that Jesus said to the crowds,

✠   **Am I a brigand, that you had to set out to cap-**
ture me with swords and clubs? I sat teaching
in the Temple day after day and you never laid
hands on me.

N   Now all this happened to fulfil the prophecies in
scripture. Then all the disciples deserted him and
ran away.
     The men who had arrested Jesus led him off to
Caiaphas the high priest, where the scribes and the
elders were assembled. Peter followed him at a distance, and when he reached the high priest's palace,
he went in and sat down with the attendants to see
what the end would be.
     The chief priests and the whole Sanhedrin were
looking for evidence against Jesus, however false, on
which they might pass the death-sentence. But they
could not find any, though several lying witnesses
came forward. Eventually two stepped forward and
made a statement,

[C] **This man said, 'I have power to destroy the**
Temple of God and in three days build it up'.

N   The high priest then stood up and said to him,

C   **Have you no answer to that? What is this**
evidence these men are bringing against you?

N   But Jesus was silent. And the high priest said to
him,

15

C   I put you on oath by the living God to tell us if 26:6 you are the Christ, the Son of God.

N   Jesus answered,

✠   **The words are your own. Moreover, I tell you that from this time onward you will see the Son of Man seated at the right hand of the Power and coming on the clouds of heaven.**

N   At this, the high priest tore his clothes and said,

C   **He has blasphemed. What need of witnesses have we now? There! You have just heard the blasphemy. What is your opinion?**

N   They answered,

[C] **He deserves to die.**

N   Then they spat in his face and hit him with their fists; others said as they struck him,

[C] **Play the prophet, Christ! Who hit you then?**

N   Meanwhile Peter was sitting outside in the courtyard, and a servant-girl came up to him and said,

C   **You too were with Jesus the Galilean.**

N   But he denied it in front of them all, saying,

C   **I do not know what you are talking about.**

N   When he went out to the gateway another servant-girl saw him and said to the people there,

C   **This man was with Jesus the Nazarene.**

N   And again, with an oath, he denied it,

C   **I do not know the man.**

N   A little later the bystanders came up and said to Peter,

[C] **You are one of them for sure! Why, your** 26:73
accent gives you away.

N   Then he started calling down curses on himself and
swearing,

C   **I do not know the man.**

N   At that moment the cock crew, and Peter remem- 26:75
bered what Jesus had said, "Before the cock crows
you will have disowned me three times." And he
went outside and wept bitterly.

When morning came, all the chief priests and the 27:1
elders of the people met in council to bring about
the death of Jesus. They had him bound, and led
him away to hand him over to Pilate, the governor.
When he found that Jesus had been condemned,
Judas his betrayer was filled with remorse and took
the thirty pieces of silver back to the chief priests and
elders, saying,

C   **I have sinned. I have betrayed innocent blood.**

N   They replied,

[C] **What is that to us? That is your concern.**

N   And flinging down the silver pieces in the sanctuary
he made off, and went and hanged himself. The
chief priests picked up the silver pieces and said,

[C] **It is against the Law to put this into the**
treasury; it is blood money.

N   So they discussed the matter and bought the potter's
field with it as a graveyard for foreigners, and this is
why the field is called the Field of Blood today. The
words of the prophet Jeremiah were then fulfilled:
And they took the thirty silver pieces, the sum at
which the precious One was priced by children of

Israel, and they gave them for the potter's field, just **27:10**
as the Lord directed me.

Jesus, then, was brought before the governor, and **27:11**
the governor put to him this question,

C **Are you the king of the Jews?**

N Jesus replied,

✠ **It is you who say it.**

N But when he was accused by the chief priests and
the elders he refused to answer at all. Pilate then
said to him,

C **Do you not hear how many charges they have
brought against you?**

N But to the governor's complete amazement, he
offered no reply to any of the charges.

At festival time it was the governor's practice to
release a prisoner for the people, anyone they chose.
Now there was at that time a notorious prisoner
whose name was Barabbas. So when the crowd
gathered, Pilate said to them,

C **Which do you want me to release for you:
Barabbas or Jesus who is called Christ?**

N For Pilate knew it was out of jealousy that they had
handed him over.

Now as he was seated in the chair of judgement,
his wife sent him a message,

C **Have nothing to do with that man; I have been
upset all day by a dream I had about him.**

N The chief priests and the elders, however, had per-
suaded the crowd to demand the release of Barabbas
and the execution of Jesus. So when the governor
spoke and asked them,

C **Which of the two do you want me to release** 27:21
   for you?

N They said,

[C] **Barabbas.**

N Pilate said to them,

C **What am I to do with Jesus who is called**
   Christ?

N They all said,

[C] **Let him be crucified!**

N Pilate asked,

C **Why? What harm has he done?**

N But they all shouted the louder,

[C] **Let him be crucified!**

N Then Pilate saw that he was making no impression,
   that in fact a riot was imminent. So he took some
   water, washed his hands in front of the crowd and
   said,

C **I am innocent of this man's blood. It is your**
   concern.

N And the people, to a man, shouted back,

[C] **His blood be on us and on our children!**

N Then he released Barabbas for them. He ordered
   Jesus to be first scourged and then handed over to
   be crucified.

   The governor's soldiers took Jesus with them into
   the Praetorium and collected the whole cohort
   round him. Then they stripped him and made him
   wear a scarlet cloak, and having twisted some
   thorns into a crown they put this on his head and

placed a reed in his right hand. To make fun of him 27:29
they knelt to him saying,

[C] **Hail, king of the Jews!**

N And they spat on him and took the reed and struck
him on the head with it. And when they had finished
making fun of him, they took off the cloak and
dressed him in his own clothes and led him away to
crucify him.

On their way out, they came across a man from
Cyrene, Simon by name, and enlisted him to carry
his cross. When they had reached a place called
Golgotha, that is, the place of the skull, they gave
him wine to drink. When they had finished crucifying him they shared out his clothing by casting lots,
and then sat down and stayed there keeping guard
over him.

Above his head was placed the charge against
him: it read: 'This is Jesus, the King of the Jews'.
At the same time two robbers were crucified with
him, one on the right and one on the left.

The passers-by jeered at him; they shook their
heads and said,

[C] **So you would destroy the Temple and rebuild
it in three days! Then save yourself! If you are
God's son, come down from the cross!**

N The chief priests, with the scribes and elders
mocked him in the same way, saying,

[C] **He saved others; he cannot save himself. He is
the King of Israel; let him come down from
the cross now, and we will believe in him. He
put his trust in God; now let God rescue him
if he wants him. For he did say, 'I am the son
of God'.**

N   Even the robbers who were crucified with him   27:44
taunted him in the same way.

     From the sixth hour there was darkness over all
the land until the ninth hour. And about the ninth
hour, Jesus cried out in a loud voice,

✠   **Eli, Eli, Lama sabachthani?**

N   That is,

✠   **'My God, my God, why have you deserted me?'**

N   When some of those who stood there heard this,
they said,

[C]   **The man is calling on Elijah,**

N   and one of them quickly ran to get a sponge which
he dipped in vinegar and, putting it on a reed, gave
it him to drink. The rest of them said,

[C]   **Wait! See if Elijah will come to save him.**

N   But Jesus, again crying out in a loud voice, yielded
up his spirit.

     At that, the veil of the Temple was torn in two
from top to bottom; the earth quaked; the rocks
were split; the tombs opened and the bodies of
many holy men rose from the dead, and these, after
his resurrection, came out of the tombs, entered the
Holy City and appeared to a number of people.
Meanwhile the centurion, together with the others   27:54
guarding Jesus, had seen the earthquake and all
that was taking place, and they were terrified and
said,

[C]   **In truth this was a son of God.**

N   And many women were there, watching from a   27:55
distance, the same women who had followed Jesus
from Galilee and looked after him. Among them

were Mary of Magdala, Mary the mother of James 27:56
and Joseph, and the mother of Zebedee's sons.

When it was evening, there came a rich man of
Arimathaea, called Joseph, who had himself become
a disciple of Jesus. This man went to Pilate and
asked for the body of Jesus. Pilate thereupon
ordered it to be handed over. So Joseph took the
body, wrapped it in a clean shroud and put it in his
own new tomb which he had hewn out of the rock.
He then rolled a large stone across the entrance of
the tomb and went away. Now Mary of Magdala 27:61
and the other Mary were there, sitting opposite the
sepulchre.

Next day, that is, when Preparation Day was
over, the chief priests and the Pharisees went in a
body to Pilate and said to him,

[C] **Your Excellency, we recall that this impostor
said, while he was still alive, 'After three days
I shall rise again'. Therefore give the order to
have the sepulchre kept secure until the third
day, for fear his disciples come and steal him
away and tell the people, 'He has risen from
the dead'. This last piece of fraud would be
worse than what went before.**

N   Pilate said to them,

C   **You may have your guards. Go and make all
as secure as you know how.**

N   So they went and made the sepulchre secure, putting seals on the stone and mounting a guard.

THIS IS THE GOSPEL OF THE LORD

The Passion of Our Lord Jesus Christ According to Mark

THE PASSION OF OUR LORD
JESUS CHRIST
ACCORDING TO MARK

[Short version: 15: 1–39]

N   It was two days before the Passover and the feast of **14:1**
    Unleavened Bread, and the chief priests and the
    scribes were looking for a way to arrest Jesus by
    some trick and have him put to death. For they
    said,

[C] **It must not be during the festivities, or there
    will be a disturbance among the people.**

N   Jesus was at Bethany in the house of Simon the
    leper; he was at dinner when a woman came in
    with an alabaster jar of very costly ointment, pure
    nard. She broke the jar and poured the ointment on
    his head. Some who were there said to one another
    indignantly,

[C] **Why this waste of ointment? Ointment like
    this could have been sold for over three hun-
    dred denarii and the money given to the poor;**

N   and they were angry with her. But Jesus said,

✠   **Leave her alone. Why are you upsetting her?
    What she has done for me is one of the good
    works. You have the poor with you always,
    and you can be kind to them whenever you**

25

wish, but you will not always have me. She has 14:8
done what was in her power to do; she has
anointed my body beforehand for its burial. I
tell you solemnly, wherever throughout all
the world the Good News is proclaimed, what
she has done will be told also, in remembrance
of her.

N Judas Iscariot, one of the Twelve, approached the
chief priests with an offer to hand Jesus over to them.
They were delighted to hear it, and promised to
give him money; and he looked for a way of betraying him when the opportunity should occur.

On the first day of Unleavened Bread, when the
Passover lamb was sacrificed, his disciples said to
him,

[C] Where do you want us to go and make the
preparations for you to eat the passover?

N So he sent two of his disciples, saying to them,

✠ Go into the city and you will meet a man
carrying a pitcher of water. Follow him, and
say to the owner of the house which he enters,
'The Master says: Where is my dining room
in which I can eat the passover with my
disciples?' He will show you a large upper
room furnished with couches, all prepared.
Make the preparations for us there.

N The disciples set out and went to the city and found
everything as he had told them, and prepared the
Passover.

When evening came he arrived with the Twelve.
And while they were at table eating, Jesus said,

✠ I tell you solemnly, one of you is about to
betray me, one of you eating with me.

N   They were distressed and asked him, one after **14:19** another,

C   **Not I, surely?**

N   He said to them,

✠   **It is one of the Twelve, one who is dipping into the same dish with me. Yes, the Son of Man is going to his fate, as the scriptures say he will, but alas for that man by whom the Son of Man is betrayed! Better for that man if he had never been born!**

N   And as they were eating he took some bread, and when he had said the blessing he broke it and gave it to them, saying,

✠   **Take it; this is my body.**

N   Then he took a cup, and when he had returned thanks he gave it to them, and all drank from it, and he said to them,

✠   **This is my blood, the blood of the covenant, which is to be poured out for many. I tell you solemnly, I shall not drink any more wine until the day I drink the new wine in the kingdom of God.**

N   After psalms had been sung they left for the Mount of Olives. And Jesus said to them,

✠   **You will all lose faith, for the scripture says, 'I shall strike the shepherd and the sheep will be scattered'. However after my resurrection I shall go before you to Galilee.**

N   Peter said,

C   **Even if all lose faith, I will not.**

N   And Jesus said to him,

✠   **I tell you solemnly, this day, this very night,** 14:30
    before the cock crows twice, you will have
    disowned me three times.

N   But he repeated still more earnestly,

C   **If I have to die with you, I will never disown**
    you.

N   And they all said the same.
     They came to a small estate called Gethsemane,
    and Jesus said to his disciples,

✠   **Stay here while I pray.**

N   Then he took Peter and James and John with him.
    And a sudden fear came over him, and great distress.
    And he said to them,

✠   **My soul is sorrowful to the point of death.**
    Wait here, and keep awake.

N   And going on a little further he threw himself on
    the ground and prayed that, if it were possible, this
    hour might pass him by. He said,

✠   **Abba (Father)! Everything is possible for you.**
    Take this cup away from me. But let it be as
    you, not I, would have it.

N   He came back and found them sleeping, and he
    said to Peter,

✠   **Simon, are you asleep? Had you not the**
    strength to keep awake one hour? You should
    be awake, and praying not to be put to the
    test. The spirit is willing but the flesh is weak.

N   Again he went away and prayed, saying the same
    words. And once more he came back and found
    them sleeping, their eyes were so heavy; and they

could find no answer for him. He came back a **14:41**
third time and said to them,

✠ **You can sleep on now and take your rest. It is
all over. The hour has come. Now the Son of
Man is to be betrayed into the hands of sinners. Get up! Let us go! My betrayer is close at
hand already.**

N Even while he was still speaking, Judas, one of the
Twelve, came up with a number of men armed with
swords and clubs, sent by the chief priests and the
scribes and the elders. Now the traitor had arranged
a signal with them. He had said,

C **'The one I kiss, he is the man. Take him in
charge, and see he is well guarded when you
lead him away.'**

N So when the traitor came, he went straight up to
Jesus and said,

C **Rabbi!**

N and kissed him. The others seized him and took him
in charge. Then one of the bystanders drew his sword
and struck out at the high priest's servant, and cut
off his ear.
   Then Jesus spoke,

✠ **Am I a brigand that you had to set out to cap-
ture me with swords and clubs? I was among
you teaching in the Temple day after day and
you never laid hands on me. But this is to fulfil
the scriptures.**

N And they all deserted him and ran away. A young
man who followed him had nothing on but a linen
cloth. They caught hold of him, but he left the cloth
in their hands and ran away naked.

They led Jesus off to the high priest; and all the **14:53** chief priests and the elders and the scribes assembled there. Peter had followed him at a distance, right into the high priest's palace, and was sitting with the attendants warming himself at the fire.

The chief priests and the whole Sanhedrin were looking for evidence against Jesus on which they might pass the death-sentence. But they could not find any. Several, indeed, brought false evidence against him, but their evidence was conflicting. Some stood up and submitted this false evidence against him,

[C] **We heard him say, 'I am going to destroy this Temple made by human hands, and in three days build another, not made by human hands'.**

N But even on this point their evidence was conflicting. The high priest then stood up before the whole assembly and put this question to Jesus,

C **Have you no answer to that? What is this evidence these men are bringing against you?**

N But he was silent and made no answer at all. The high priest put a second question to him,

C **Are you the Christ the Son of the Blessed One?**

N Jesus said,

✠ **I am, and you will see the Son of Man seated at the right hand of the Power and coming with the clouds of heaven.**

N The high priest tore his robes, and said,

C **What need of witnesses have we now? You heard the blasphemy. What is your finding?**

30

N And they all gave their verdict: he deserved to die. **14:64**
   Some of them started spitting at him and, blind-
   folding him, began hitting him with their fists and
   shouting,

[C] **Play the prophet!**

N And the attendants rained blows on him.
      While Peter was down below in the courtyard,
   one of the high-priest's servant-girls came up. She
   saw Peter warming himself there, stared at him and
   said,

C **You too were with Jesus, the man from
   Nazareth.**

N But he denied it, saying

C **I do not know, I do not understand what you
   are talking about.**

N And he went out into the forecourt. The servant-
   girl saw him and again started telling the bystanders,

C **This fellow is one of them.**

N But he again denied it. A little later the bystanders
   themselves said to Peter,

[C] **You are one of them for sure! Why, you are a
   Galilean.**

N But he started calling curses on himself and swearing,

C **I do not know the man you speak of.**

N At that moment the cock crew for the second time, **14:72**
   and Peter recalled how Jesus had said to him,
   'Before the cock crows twice, you will have disowned
   me three times'. And he burst into tears.
      First thing in the morning, the chief priest to- **15:1**
   gether with the elders and scribes, in short the whole

Sanhedrin, had their plan ready. They had Jesus 15:1
bound and took him away and handed him over to
Pilate.

Pilate questioned him,

C Are you the king of the Jews?

N He answered,

✠ It is you who say it,

N And the chief priests brought many accusations
against him. Pilate questioned him again,

C Have you no reply at all? See how many accusations they are bringing against you!

N But to Pilate's amazement, Jesus made no further
reply.

At festival time Pilate used to release a prisoner
for them, anyone they asked for. Now a man called
Barabbas was then in prison with the rioters who
had committed murder during the uprising. When
the crowd went up and began to ask Pilate the cus-
tomary favour, Pilate answered them,

C Do you want me to release for you the king of
the Jews?

N For he realised it was out of jealousy that the chief
priests had handed Jesus over. The chief priests,
however, had incited the crowd to demand that he
should release Barabbas for them instead. Then
Pilate spoke again.

C But in that case, what am I to do with the man
you call king of the Jews?

N They shouted back,

[C] Crucify him!

N Pilate asked them,

C   **Why? What harm has he done?**   **15:14**

N   But they shouted all the louder,

[C] **Crucify him!**

N   So Pilate, anxious to placate the crowd, released
    Barabbas for them and, having ordered Jesus to be
    scourged, handed him over to be crucified.
    The soldiers led him away to the inner part of the
    palace, that is, the Praetorium, and called the
    whole cohort together. They dressed him up in
    purple, twisted some thorns into a crown and put it
    on him. And they began saluting him,

[C] **Hail, king of the Jews!**

N   They struck his head with a reed and spat on him;
    and they went down on their knees to do him
    homage. And when they had finished making fun of
    him, they took off the purple and dressed him in his
    own clothes.
    They led him out to crucify him. They enlisted a
    passerby, Simon of Cyrene, father of Alexander and
    Rufus, who was coming in from the country, to
    carry his cross. They brought Jesus to the place
    called Golgotha, which means the place of the skull.
    They offered him wine mixed with myrrh, but he
    refused it. Then they crucified him, and shared out
    his clothing, casting lots to decide what each should
    get. It was the third hour when they crucified him.
    The inscription giving the charge against him read:
    'The King of the Jews.' And they crucified two
    robbers with him, one on his right and one on his
    left.
    The passers-by jeered at him; they shook their
    heads and said,

[C] **Aha! So you would destroy the Temple and**

33

rebuild it in three days! Then save yourself: 15:3
come down from the cross!

N   The chief priests and the scribes mocked him among themselves in the same way. They said,

[C] **He saved others, he cannot save himself. Let the Christ, the king of Israel, come down from the cross now, for us to see it and believe.**

N   Even those who were crucified with him taunted him.

     When the sixth hour came there was darkness over the whole land until the ninth hour. And at the ninth hour Jesus cried out in a loud voice,

✠ **Eloi, Eloi, lama sabachthani?**

N   This means

✠ **'My God, my God, why have you deserted me?'**

N   When some of those who stood by heard this, they said,

[C] **Listen, he is calling on Elijah.**

N   Someone ran and soaked a sponge in vinegar and, putting it on a reed, gave it him to drink, saying,

C   **Wait and see if Elijah will come to take him down.**

N   But Jesus gave a loud cry and breathed his last. And the veil of the Temple was torn in two from top to bottom. The centurion, who was standing in front 15:39
of him, had seen how he had died, and he said,

C   **In truth this man was a son of God.**

N   There were some women watching from a distance. 15:40
Among them were Mary of Magdala, Mary who was the mother of James the younger, and Joset, and

Salome. These used to follow him and look after 15:41
him when he was in Galilee. And there were many
other women there who had come up to Jerusalem
with him.

It was now evening, and since it was Preparation
Day (that is, the vigil of the sabbath), there came
Joseph of Arimathaea, a prominent member of the
Council, who himself lived in the hope of seeing the
kingdom of God, and he boldly went to Pilate and
asked for the body of Jesus. Pilate, astonished that
he should have died so soon, summoned the centurion and enquired if he was already dead. Having
been assured of this by the centurion, he granted
the corpse to Joseph who bought a shroud, took
Jesus down from the cross, wrapped him in the
shroud and laid him in a tomb which had been
hewn out of the rock. He then rolled a stone against
the entrance to the tomb. Mary of Magdala and
Mary the mother of Joset were watching and took
note of where he was laid.

THIS IS THE GOSPEL OF THE LORD

The Passion of Our Lord Jesus Christ According to Luke

CHAPTER 22, VERSES 1–13*

N   The feast of Unleavened Bread, called the Passover, was **22:1** now drawing near, and the chief priests and the scribes were looking for some way of doing away with him, because they mistrusted the people.

    Then Satan entered into Judas, surnamed Iscariot, who was numbered among the Twelve. He went to the chief priests and the officers of the guard to discuss a scheme for handing Jesus over to them. They were delighted and agreed to give him money. He accepted, and looked for an opportunity to betray him to them without the people knowing.

    The day of Unleavened Bread came round, the day on which the passover had to be sacrificed, and Jesus sent Peter and John, saying,

✠   **Go and make the preparations for us to eat the passover.**

N   They asked,

[C]   **Where do you want us to prepare it?**

N   He said

✠   **Listen, as you go into the city you will meet a man** **22:11** **carrying a pitcher of water. Follow him into the house he enters and tell the owner of the house, 'The Master has this to say to you: Where is the dining room in which I can eat the passover with my disciples?' The man will show you a large upper room furnished with couches. Make preparations there.**

N   They set off and found everything as he had told them, and prepared the Passover.

       * Used in the Church of England as Introduction to the Passion.

THE PASSION OF OUR LORD
JESUS CHRIST
ACCORDING TO LUKE

[Short version 23:1—23:49]

N   When the hour came Jesus took his place at **22:14** table, and the apostles with him. And he said to them,

✠   **I have longed to eat this passover with you before I suffer; because, I tell you, I shall not eat it again until it is fulfilled in the kingdom of God.**

N   Then, taking a cup, he gave thanks and said,

✠   **Take this and share it among you, because from now on, I tell you, I shall not drink wine until the kingdom of God comes.**

N   Then he took some bread, and when he had given thanks, broke it and gave it to them, saying,

✠   **This is my body which will be given for you; do this as a memorial of me.**

N   He did the same with the cup after supper, and said,

✠   **This cup is the new covenant in my blood which will be poured out for you.**
   And yet, here with me on the table is the hand of the man who betrays me. The Son of Man does indeed go to his fate even as it has been decreed, but alas for that man by whom he is betrayed!

N   And they began to ask one another which of them it could be who was to do this thing.

A dispute arose also between them about which 22:24
should be reckoned the greatest, but he said to them,

✠ **Among pagans it is the kings who lord it over
them, and those who have authority over them
are given the title Benefactor. This must not
happen with you. No; the greatest among you
must behave as if he were the youngest, the
leader as if he were the one who serves. For
who is the greater: the one at table or the one
who serves? The one at table, surely? Yet here
am I among you as one who serves!**

**You are the men who have stood by me
faithfully in my trials; and now I confer a
kingdom on you, just as my Father conferred
one on me: you will eat and drink at my table
in my kingdom, and you will sit on thrones to
judge the twelve tribes of Israel.**

**Simon, Simon! Satan, you must know, has
got his wish to sift you all like wheat; but I
have prayed for you, Simon, that your faith
may not fail, and once you have recovered,
you in your turn must strengthen your
brothers.**

N   He answered,

C   **Lord, I would be ready to go to prison with
you, and to death.**

N   Jesus replied,

✠ **I tell you, Peter, by the time the cock crows
today you will have denied three times that
you know me.**

N   He said to them,

✠ **When I sent you out without purse or haversack or sandals, were you short of anything?**

N   They answered,   22:36

[C] **No.**

N   He said to them,

✠ **But now if you have a purse, take it: if you have a haversack, do the same; if you have no sword, sell your cloak and buy one, because I tell you these words of scripture have to be fulfilled in me: He let himself be taken for a criminal. Yes, what scripture says about me is even now reaching its fulfilment.**

N   They said,   22:38

[C] **Lord, there are two swords here now.**

N   He said to them,

✠ **That is enough!**

N   He then left the upper room to make his way as 22:39 usual to the Mount of Olives, with the disciples following. When they reached the place he said to them,

✠ **Pray not to be put to the test.**

N   Then he withdrew from them, about a stone's throw away, and knelt down and prayed, saying,

✠ **Father, if you are willing, take this cup away from me. Nevertheless, let your will be done, not mine.**

N   Then an angel appeared to him coming from heaven to give him strength. In his anguish he prayed even more earnestly, and his sweat fell to the ground like great drops of blood.

    When he rose from prayer he went to the disciples and found them sleeping for sheer grief. He said to them,

✠ **Why are you asleep? Get up and pray not to be 22:46 put to the test.**

N He was still speaking when a number of men appeared, and at the head of them the man called Judas, one of the Twelve, who went up to Jesus to kiss him. Jesus said,

✠ **Judas, are you betraying the Son of Man with a kiss?**

N His followers, seeing what was happening, said,

[C] **Lord, shall we use our swords?**

N And one of them struck out at the high priest's servant, and cut off his right ear. But at this Jesus spoke,

✠ **Leave off! That will do!**

N And touching the man's ear he healed him.
    Then Jesus spoke to the chief priests and captains of the Temple guard and elders who had come for him. He said,

✠ **Am I a brigand that you had to set out with swords and clubs? When I was among you in the Temple day after day you never moved to lay hands on me. But this is your hour; this is the reign of darkness.**

N They seized him then and led him away, and they took him to the high priest's house. Peter followed at a distance. They had lit a fire in the middle of the courtyard and Peter sat down among them, and as he was sitting there by the blaze a servant-girl saw him, peered at him and said,

C **This person was with him too.**

N But he denied it, saying,

C **Woman, I do not know him.**   **22**:57

N Shortly afterwards, someone else saw him and said,

C **You are another of them.**

N But Peter replied,

C **I am not, my friend.**

N About an hour later another man insisted saying,

C **This fellow was certainly with him. Why, he is a Galilean.**

N Peter said,

C **My friend, I do not know what you are talking about.**

N At that instant, while he was still speaking, the cock crew, and the Lord turned and looked straight at Peter, and Peter remembered what the Lord had said to him, 'Before the cock crows today, you will have disowned me three times'. And he went outside and wept bitterly.

  Meanwhile the men who guarded Jesus were mocking and beating him. They blindfolded him and questioned him, saying,

[C] **Play the prophet. Who hit you then?**

N And they continued heaping insults on him.

  When day broke there was a meeting of the elders of the people, attended by the chief priests and scribes. He was brought before their council, and they said to him,

[C] **If you are the Christ, tell us.**

N He replied,

✠ **If I tell you, you will not believe me, and if I question you, you will not answer. But from**

now on, the Son of Man will be seated at the 22:69
right hand of the Power of God.

N   Then they all said,

[C]   So you are the Son of God then?

N   He answered,

✠   It is you who say I am.

N   They said,   22:71

[C]   What need of witnesses have we now? We
have heard it for ourselves from his own lips.

N   The whole assembly then rose, and they brought him 23:1
before Pilate.
     They began their accusation by saying,

[C]   We found this man inciting our people to
revolt, opposing payment of tribute to Caesar,
and claiming to be Christ, a king.

N   Pilate put to him this question,

C   Are you the king of the Jews?

N   He replied,

✠   It is you who say it.

N   Pilate then said to the chief priests and the crowd,

C   I find no case against this man.

N   But they persisted,

[C]   He is inflaming the people with his teaching
all over Judaea; it has come all the way from
Galilee, where he started, down to here.

N   When Pilate heard this, he asked if the man were a
Galilean; and finding that he came under Herod's
jurisdiction he passed him over to Herod who was
also in Jerusalem at that time.

Herod was delighted to see Jesus; he had heard **23**:8 about him and had been wanting for a long time to set eyes on him; moreover, he was hoping to see some miracle worked by him. So he questioned him at some length; but without getting any reply. Meanwhile the chief priests and the scribes were there, violently pressing their accusations. Then Herod, together with his guards, treated him with contempt and made fun of him; he put a rich cloak on him and sent him back to Pilate. And though Herod and Pilate had been enemies before, they were reconciled that same day.

Pilate then summoned the chief priests and the leading men and the people. He said,

C **You brought this man before me as a political agitator. Now I have gone into the matter myself in your presence and found no case against him. Nor has Herod either, since he has sent him back to us. As you can see, the man has done nothing that deserves death, so I shall have him flogged and then let him go.**

N But as one man they howled,

[C] **Away with him! Give us Barabbas!**

N This man had been thrown into prison for causing a riot in the city and for murder.

Pilate was anxious to set Jesus free and addressed them again, but they shouted back.

[C] **Crucify him! Crucify him!**

N And for the third time he spoke to them,

C **Why? What harm has this man done? I have found no case against him that deserves death, so I shall have him punished and then let him go.**

45

N   But they kept on shouting at the top of their voices, **23:23** demanding that he should be crucified. And their shouts were growing louder.

     Pilate then gave his verdict: their demand was to be granted. He released the man they asked for, who had been imprisoned for rioting and murder, and handed Jesus over to them to deal with as they pleased.

     As they were leading him away they seized on a man, Simon from Cyrene, who was coming in from the country, and made him shoulder the cross and carry it behind Jesus. Large numbers of people followed him, and of women too, who mourned and lamented for him. But Jesus turned to them and said,

✠   **Daughters of Jerusalem, do not weep for me; weep rather for yourselves and for your children. For the days will surely come when people will say, 'Happy are those who are barren, the wombs that have never borne, the breasts that have never suckled!' Then they will begin to say to the mountains, 'Fall on us!'; to the hills, 'Cover us!' For if men use the green wood like this, what will happen when it is dry?**

N   Now with him they were also leading out two other criminals to be executed.

     When they reached the place called The Skull, they crucified him there and the two criminals also, one on the right, the other on the left. Jesus said,

✠   **Father, forgive them; they do not know what they are doing.**

N   Then they cast lots to share out his clothing. The people stayed there watching him. As for the leaders, they jeered at him, saying,

[C] **He saved others; let him save himself if he is** 23:35
the Christ of God, the Chosen One.

N The soldiers mocked him too, and when they approached to offer him vinegar they said,

[C] **If you are the king of the Jews, save yourself.**

N Above him there was an inscription: 'This is the King of the Jews.'
One of the criminals hanging there abused him, saying,

C **Are you not the Christ? Save yourself and us as well.**

N But the other spoke up and rebuked him.

C **Have you no fear of God at all? You got the same sentence as he did, but in our case we deserved it: we are paying for what we did. But this man has done nothing wrong. Jesus, remember me when you come into your kingdom.**

N He replied

✠ **Indeed, I promise you, today you will be with me in paradise.**

N It was now about the sixth hour and, with the sun eclipsed, a darkness came over the whole land until the ninth hour. The veil of the Temple was torn right down the middle; and when Jesus had cried out in a loud voice, he said,

✠ **Father, into your hands I commit my spirit.**

N With these words he breathed his last.
When the centurion saw what had taken place, **23:47**
he gave praise to God and said,

C **This was a great and good man.** 23:47

N   And when all the people who had gathered for the 23:48
spectacle saw what had happened, they went home
beating their breasts.

All his friends stood at a distance; so also did the 23:49
women who had accompanied him from Galilee,
and they saw all this happen.

Then a member of the council arrived, an upright
and virtuous man named Joseph. He had not con-
sented to what the others had planned and carried
out. He came from Arimathaea, a Jewish town, and
he lived in the hope of seeing the kingdom of God.
This man went to Pilate and asked for the body of
Jesus. He then took it down, wrapped it in a shroud
and put him in a tomb which was hewn in stone in
which no one had yet been laid. It was Preparation
Day and the sabbath was imminent.

Meanwhile the women who had come from 23:55
Galilee with Jesus were following behind. They took
note of the tomb and of the position of the body.

Then they returned and prepared spices and 23:56
ointments. And on the sabbath day they rested, as
the Law required.

THIS IS THE GOSPEL OF THE LORD

The Passion of Our Lord Jesus Christ According to John

THE PASSION OF OUR LORD
JESUS CHRIST
ACCORDING TO JOHN

N Jesus left with his disciples and crossed the Kedron   18:1
valley. There was a garden there, and he went into
it with his disciples. Judas the traitor knew the place
well, since Jesus had often met his disciples there,
and he brought the cohort to this place together
with a detachment of guards sent by the chief
priests and the Pharisees, all with lanterns and
torches and weapons. Knowing everything that was
going to happen to him, Jesus then came forward
and said,

✠ **Who are you looking for?**

N They answered,

[C] **Jesus the Nazarene.**

N He said,

✠ **I am he.**

N Now Judas the traitor was standing among them.
When Jesus said, 'I am he', they moved back and
fell to the ground. He asked them a second time,

✠ **Who are you looking for?**

N They said,

[C] **Jesus the Nazarene.**   18:5

N   Jesus replied

✠   **I have told you that I am he. If I am the one you are looking for, let these others go.**

N   This was to fulfil the words he had spoken: 'Not one of those you gave me have I lost'.
     Simon Peter, who carried a sword, drew it and wounded the high priest's servant, cutting off his right ear. The servant's name was Malchus. Jesus said to Peter,

✠   **Put your sword back in its scabbard; am I not to drink the cup that the Father has given me?**

N   The cohort and its captain and the Jewish guards seized Jesus and bound him. They took him first to Annas, because Annas was the father-in-law of Caiaphas, who was high priest that year. It was Caiaphas who had suggested to the Jews, 'It is better for one man to die for the people'.
     Simon Peter, with another disciple, followed Jesus. This disciple, who was known to the high priest, went with Jesus into the high priest's palace. but Peter stayed outside the door. So the other disciple, the one known to the high priest, went out, spoke to the woman who was keeping the door and brought Peter in. The maid on duty at the door said to Peter,

C   **Aren't you another of that man's disciples?**

N   He answered,

C   **I am not.**

N   Now it was cold, and the servants and guards had lit a charcoal fire and were standing there warming

themselves; so Peter stood there too, warming him- 18:18
self with the others.

The high priest questioned Jesus about his
disciples and his teaching. Jesus answered,

✠ **I have spoken openly for all the world to hear;
I have always taught in the synagogue and in
the Temple where all the Jews meet together:
I have said nothing in secret. But why ask me?
Ask my hearers what I taught: they know
what I said.**

N At these words, one of the guards standing by gave
Jesus a slap in the face, saying,

C **Is that the way to answer the high priest?**

N Jesus replied,

✠ **If there is something wrong in what I said,
point it out; but if there is no offence in it, why
do you strike me?**

N Then Annas sent him, still bound, to Caiaphas, the
high priest.

As Simon Peter stood there warming himself,
someone said to him,

C **Aren't you another of his disciples?**

N He denied it saying,

C **I am not.**

N One of the high priest's servants, a relation of the
man whose ear Peter had cut off, said,

C **Didn't I see you in the garden with him?**

N Again Peter denied it; and at once a cock crew.

They then led Jesus from the house of Caiaphas to
the Praetorium. It was now morning. They did not
go into the Praetorium themselves or they would be

defiled and unable to eat the passover. So Pilate 18:29
came outside to them and said,

C   **What charge do you bring against this man?**

N   They replied,

[C] **If he were not a criminal, we should not be
handing him over to you.**

N   Pilate said,

C   **Take him yourselves, and try him by your
own Law.**

N   The Jews answered,

[C] **We are not allowed to put a man to death.**

N   This was to fulfil the words Jesus had spoken indi-
cating the way he was going to die.
    So Pilate went back into the Praetorium and
called Jesus to him, and asked,

C   **Are you the king of the Jews?**

N   Jesus replied,

✠   **Do you ask this of your own accord, or have
others spoken to you about me?**

N   Pilate answered,

C   **Am I a Jew? It is your own people and the
chief priests who have handed you over to me:
what have you done?**

N   Jesus replied,

✠   **Mine is not a kingdom of this world; if my
kingdom were of this world, my men would
have fought to prevent me being surrendered
to the Jews. But my kingdom is not of this
kind.**

N   Pilate said,   **18**:37

C   **So you are a king then?**

N   Jesus answered,

✠   **It is you who say it. Yes, I am a King. I was born for this, I came into the world for this; to bear witness to my truth, and all who are on the side of truth listen to my voice.**

N   Pilate said

C   **Truth? What is that?**

N   And with that he went out again to the Jews and said,

C   **I find no case against him. But according to a custom of yours I should release one prisoner at the Passover; would you like me, then, to release the king of the Jews?**

N   At this they shouted:

[C]   **Not this man, but Barabbas.**

N   Barabbas was a brigand.
      Pilate then had Jesus taken away and scourged;   **19**:1 and after this, the soldiers twisted some thorns into a crown and put it on his head, and dressed him in a purple robe. They kept coming up to him and saying,

[C]   **Hail, king of the Jews!**

N   and they slapped him in the face.
      Pilate came outside again and said to them,

C   **Look, I am going to bring him out to you to let you see that I find no case.**

N   Jesus then came out wearing the crown of thorns and the purple robe. Pilate said,

C   **Here is the man.**

N   When they saw him the chief priests and the guards shouted,

[C] **Crucify him! Crucify him!**

N   Pilate said,

C   **Take him yourselves and crucify him: I can find no case against him.**

N   The Jews replied,

[C] **We have a Law, and according to the Law he ought to die, because he has claimed to be the Son of God.**

N   When Pilate heard them say this his fears increased. Re-entering the Praetorium, he said to Jesus,

C   **Where do you come from?**

N   But Jesus made no answer. Pilate then said to him,

C   **Are you refusing to speak to me? Surely you know I have power to release you and I have power to crucify you?**

N   Jesus replied

✠   **You would have no power over me if it had not been given you from above; that is why the one who handed me over to you has the greater guilt.**

N   From that moment Pilate was anxious to set him free, but the Jews shouted.

[C] **If you set him free you are no friend of Caesar's; anyone who makes himself king is defying Caesar.**

N   Hearing these words, Pilate had Jesus brought out, and seated himself on the chair of judgement at a

place called the Pavement, in Hebrew Gabbatha. **19:13**
It was Passover Preparation Day, about the sixth
hour. Pilate said to the Jews,

C   **Here is your king.**

N   They said,

[C] **Take him away, take him away. Crucify him!**

N   Pilate said,

C   **Do you want me to crucify your king?**

N   The chief priests answered,

[C] **We have no king except Caesar.**

N   So in the end Pilate handed him over to them to be
crucified.
    They then took charge of Jesus, and carrying his
own cross he went out of the city to the place of the
skull, or, as it was called in Hebrew, Golgotha,
where they crucified him with two others, one on
either side with Jesus in the middle. Pilate wrote out
a notice and had it fixed to the cross; it ran: 'Jesus
the Nazarene, King of the Jews.' This notice was
read by many of the Jews, because the place where
Jesus was crucified was not far from the city, and
the writing was in Hebrew, Latin and Greek. So the
Jewish chief priests said to Pilate,

[C] **You should not write 'King of the Jews', but
'This man said: I am King of the Jews'.**

N   Pilate answered,

C   **What I have written, I have written.**

N   When the soldiers had finished crucifying Jesus they
took his clothing and divided it into four shares, one
for each soldier. His undergarment was seamless,

woven in one piece from neck to hem; so they said **19:24** to one another,

[C] **Instead of tearing it, let's throw dice to decide who is to have it.**

N In this way the words of scripture were fulfilled:
They shared out my clothing among them.
They cast lots for my clothes.

This is exactly what the soldiers did.

Near the cross of Jesus stood his mother and his mother's sister, Mary the wife of Clopas, and Mary of Magdala. Seeing his mother and the disciple he loved standing near her, Jesus said to his mother,

✠ **Woman, this is your son.**

N Then to the disciple he said,

✠ **This is your mother.**

N And from that moment the disciple made a place for her in his home.

After this, Jesus knew that everything had now been completed, and to fulfil the scripture perfectly he said:

✠ **I am thirsty.**

N A jar full of vinegar stood there, so putting a sponge soaked in vinegar on a hyssop stick they held it up to his mouth. After Jesus had taken the vinegar he said,

✠ **It is accomplished;**

N and bowing his head he gave up the spirit.

It was Preparation Day, and to prevent the bodies remaining on the cross during the sabbath—since that sabbath was a day of special solemnity—the Jews asked Pilate to have the legs broken and the

bodies taken away. Consequently the soldiers came **19:32**
and broke the legs of the first man who had been
crucified with him and then of the other. When they
came to Jesus, they found that he was already dead,
and so instead of breaking his legs one of the soldiers
pierced his side with a lance; and immediately there
came out blood and water. This is the evidence of
one who saw it—trustworthy evidence, and he
knows he speaks the truth—and he gives it so that
you may believe as well. Because all this happened
to fulfil the words of scripture:

Not one bone of his will be broken,

and again, in another place scripture says: **19:37**
They will look on the one whom they have pierced.

After this, Joseph of Arimathaea, who was a **19:38**
disciple of Jesus—though a secret one because he
was afraid of the Jews—asked Pilate to let him
remove the body of Jesus. Pilate gave permission, so
they came and took it away. Nicodemus came as
well—the same one who had first come to Jesus at
night-time—and he brought a mixture of myrrh
and aloes, weighing about a hundred pounds. They
took the body of Jesus and wrapped it with the
spices in linen cloths, following the Jewish burial
custom. At the place where he had been crucified
there was a garden, and in this garden a new tomb
in which no one had yet been buried. Since it was
the Jewish Day of Preparation and the tomb was
near at hand, they laid Jesus there.

THIS IS THE GOSPEL OF THE LORD